TIME TO THINK:
MEDITATION AND REFLECTION

MICHAEL E. PAYTON, MA

authorHOUSE

AuthorHouse™
1663 Liberty Drive
Bloomington, IN 47403
www.authorhouse.com
Phone: 833-262-8899

Published by AuthorHouse 05/27/2022

ISBN: 978-1-6655-5872-3 (sc)
ISBN: 978-1-6655-5871-6 (e)

CONTENTS

DEDICATION

This book is dedicated to Hudson, Layla, and Liam Tyler Kurtz. Although we didn't have the opportunity to meet here, one day we will meet in a much better place but know now that my love for all three of you has never been stronger.

FOREWORD

There's nothing that pleases me more than being around happy, motivated people.

When I decided to write this book, I wanted it to be about more than just my thoughts on motivation. It was my goal to bring motivational and creative thinking to readers from some of the world's most influential and successful people.

Over the past two years I have researched the motivational efforts of some of the world's most successful and creative people coming from business, government, entertainment, sports, education, science, writers, clergy and artists. Some of these people lived centuries ago and others are living today.

I have selected memorable motivational quotes from these individuals and then offered my thoughts on those quotes.

Although the concept of this book may be unique I think it's purpose is more important. It's interesting to note that the quotations from each of these people, some separated by generations, still illustrate the common positive attitude and desire shared by all for success.

Positive and progressive thinking ignites the motivation required for success. Regardless of your profession or lifestyle, positive thinking, high self-esteem and a strong motivational force will produce a successful and healthy life.

It's my hope as you read this book that you will be inspired by the attitude of those who are credited with the quotes in such a way your life is motivated to great success.

CHAPTER 1

"You can't live a perfect day without doing something for someone who will never be able to repay you." John Wooden.

My parents used to tell me to always try to help someone any time I could because the day may come when I may need help.

I will always be grateful to my parents for that among many other things they taught me. But I've also learned another valuable lesson: real help doesn't expect reward.

I suppose one of the reasons I've always tried to be helpful to others is because of my parents. I have no problem giving them credit for it. But really, I think there was a more important lesson, one I didn't realize until several years ago. The lesson of compassion.

Compassion for your fellow man may be a quality born into all of us. Who doesn't hurt seeing news stories of people's homes burning in horrid forest fires, brutal tornadoes and destructive hurricanes?

The act of helping others is admirable and rewarding. But it should be rewarding for its results. Not from any expected gratitude later shown by those helped.

I've found one of the best feelings in the world is to know I've helped someone else. (Actually, I feel best when I've helped people who never knew I ever helped) And I know if I was expecting anything back that feeling could never have been the same.

Helping others just makes me feel good. And when I feel good, I know I'm more enjoyable to be around. It really means when I help others the immediate payback is how good I feel about myself.

You might be surprised how many people you've helped in life who may never say thank you but if you stop and think about it you realize how good you felt doing it. Holding the door open for the person following you in, picking up something someone has dropped, letting an older person in front of you in a grocery store line. These and similar acts are helping.

Expectations of reward for helping takes away any real value you may feel. It also hardens your feelings of compassion and caring. Those feelings come from the heart and expecting the wallet to grow before you offer help is not a feeling from within.

The rule of thumb my parents gave me is advice I encourage others to go by: help others and don't expect anything. Help from the heart.

CHAPTER 2

"People often say that motivation doesn't last...neither does baths. That's why we do it daily". Zig Ziglar.

Motivation is key to any action, whether negative or positive.

History is full of people who were great motivators. Keep in mind I'm not saying they were all great people but certainly great motivators

Motivation can occur in many ways under many different conditions.

I think the greatest motivator of all time was Jesus Christ. His entire life and death motivated millions and generations to Christianity.

For the most part today's "motivators" rely on holding some "carrot" or reward for the desired result.

Probably the worst successful motivation techniques involve fear. People are motivated to perform it or face loss of pay, job or some other "punishment."

I remember in school students were motivated (although I looked at it then and now) by fear of being paddled or some other humiliation in front of the class.

However there is good motivation as well. Today my biggest motivation to do the right things is my grandchildren. They motivate me and give me energy in ways I never dreamed possible.

The illustration about my grandchildren is my way of pointing out that love is a major motivator. Think about it. We do the most for those we love.

I consider many successful business leaders to be great motivators. The same with successful coaches. If you find a successful organization or continually successful sports teams you are going to find great motivators in leadership roles.

Something to remember is great leaders lead through motivation. Bosses lead through intimidation.

One final point involves self-motivation. Motivating self requires not feeling sorry for self. Emphasize the positive in your life. A little exercise I tell my students to do each day is when you first get up each morning while you're having that first cup of coffee or taking your morning jog is make a mental or written list of five blessings in your life. Do it each morning and think about how grateful you are for them. It's a great way to jump-start your day.

CHAPTER 3

"There are no limits to what you can accomplish, except the limits you place on your own thinking." Brian Tracy

I suppose it is human nature to believe we all have limitations but is it really true?

There definitely are some things that may involve certain physical requirements we all don't have. Certain jobs have strength requirements. Other jobs might require specific height requirements or for 20/20 vision. Age is also a requirement for certain employment. The point I'm making is there are some situations that are out of our hands.

How often do you let your mind limit your actions? Do you talk yourself out of things?

It's become sort of a running joke in my family that I can go into a store, pick something out to buy and if I don't go directly to the checkout lane and pay for it but do some more shopping first I will put the item back on the shelf before I leave the store. I will have talked myself out of buying it. My mind limits what I buy!

We all go through periods when we start thinking we are not good enough or we don't need certain things, relationships, etc. Its normal that our minds try to set limits using guilt, intimidation or even love to curb our actions.

Some of the greatest events in our history would never occur if we had let our minds limit our potential. The cure for epidemic diseases, man setting foot on the moon, the internet, television. The list can be endless.

I tend to believe the human mind, the brain, may very well be the most powerful organ in our body. It can control our happiness, who we form relationships with, where we live and what lifestyle we choose. In many cases I believe it controls when we want to live and when we want to die.

So how do we control our minds? Some of us turn to our Lord and Savior Jesus Christ. Some turn to clinical counselors, friends or co-workers. And unfortunately, many turn to drugs, alcohol and other things which only lead to more problems giving our minds even more power over us.

Remember that the human potential is unlimited. The more we can find ways to keep our minds from limiting our potential the more exciting, successful and promising our future.

CHAPTER 4

"To forgive is to set someone free and discover that the prisoner was you." Lewis B. Smedes.

Here is a question I like to ask my students: "Is it easier to forgive someone else or yourself?"

Forgiving others is usually the answer. Most people are harder on themselves than anyone else. I like to look at it as a trait built in at birth.

When I was coaching I knew a lot of fellow coaches, men and women, who never slept nights, lost large amounts of weight and even had relationship issues because their teams were not winning and they placed sole blame on themselves. They become distant from family and friends, became neurotic from not getting any rest and either pretty much quit eating or ate everything in sight.

People in health care fields, business and public service jobs (law enforcement, fire fighters, first responders) many times retire early because of ulcers or some other health issue due to stress brought on not by the work itself but stress brought on due to self-imposed feelings for either making a unavoidable mistake or believing they didn't try harder.

When I was in college I saw many students who could never forgive themselves if they missed a question on a test or failed a course.

The point I'm trying to make is we put undeserved pressure on ourselves for what are many times unavoidable situations. And many times these are situations where we would forgive someone else for doing the same thing.

On a more serious example, how many parents do you know blame themselves for their children's behavior as adults and in many cases even use their "bad parenting" as an excuse for that behavior.

And how many of us blame ourselves for a loved one's accident, injury or even death?

In order to not live a life of feeling responsible for everything that goes wrong in the world you must come to the realization that the world doesn't revolve only around you.

There's nothing wrong with having self-worth and believing you are important. In fact it's a goal every motivation speaker wants to achieve.

But having self-worth and believing you are responsible for everything that goes on in the world are certainly two very different things.

Forgiveness is a great gift you can freely give to anyone who has in any way wronged you or a friend. It is a great medicine that makes that person and you feel great.

So my question to you is, "why won't you give yourself the same medicine?" Why are you afraid to make yourself feel better?

By not forgiving yourself you are only punishing yourself. So, is whatever caused you to put yourself in a prison of guilt worth keeping you a prisoner or is it time to set yourself free?

CHAPTER 5

"People will forget what you said; People will forget what you did;
People will never forget how you made them feel." Maya Angelo

Are you concerned about making your "mark" in life? Do you worry about leaving a legacy?

I don't recall any time in my life when I specifically sat down and thought about how I want to be remembered.

What has surprised me over the years is how many people really do worry about what others will think about them after they are gone.

There are many people who go out of their way to leave a lasting legacy. Financial donations or support for different charities, scholarships with the assurance the family name will always be associated perpetually are one of the more common ways legacies are cemented.

Some people are remembered for athletic records: home runs, points scored, times set in races, etc.

Of course some people are remembered for things they may not want to be such as going to the electric chair.

I've found that particularly with former students and folks who were constituents while I was in public office that it wasn't so much what I did for them but how I made them feel.

One of my biggest vices has always been not listening enough. I have tried hard over the years to listen to what people are saying. In politics, in classes and in clinical work people have a lot to say. And nothing makes an individual feel more important than when they know someone is listening to them.

People feel good and feel important if what they are saying is being listened to. Keep in mind I am saying listened to, not necessarily that it has to be acted on.

People who are listened to know you value their opinion. It's the same with our children. Children want our attention. They feel valued when they know they are being listened to.

I would never be critical of anyone's motives for doing some charitable work or donating money or property or anything else. But when people know you are valuing them by giving them your attention it's a good bet they will remember. Maybe not what was even said but they remember you for listening, for recognizing them as individuals with thoughts and opinions but mostly for giving them respect.

If you really want to be remembered, don't worry so much about what you say or do for people but give them respect and dignity.

That is a feeling they will never forget.

CHAPTER 6

"You're always one choice away from changing your life." Mac Anderson

Choices are something we are all faced with every day. Some choices are simple, quick and many we don't even remember. Other choices are a whole different story. They are complex, take time to decide and are long-lasting.

Being a history buff I've always been fascinated by choices made in the past. How would our lives be affected today if Lincoln chose not to challenge the Confederacy? Where would we be if President Kennedy didn't choose to go to the moon. What might have happened if Truman chose not to drop the bombs?

Choices map the paths of our lives. The only people responsible for the choices we make is us. We map the path we take.

Unfortunately there is no training ground for making choices. Many choices we make are done without consideration of consequences. We make many choices based purely on spur of the moment impulses. We don't consider how some choices we make affect our children, our spouses, friends or ourselves.

As human beings we have the inherent right to make our own choices on how we live. As citizens of this great country we are guaranteed the right to make choices via the Bill of Rights.

I think it is crucial to remember one important fact when making choices: choices have consequences. Consequences to yourself, your family, your friends, co-workers and possibly even some people you don't even currently know.

So remember when you make choices in your life, they're not just choices that affect you. Make your choices carefully and wisely in life. Choice is a privilege but as with other privileges it comes with responsibility.

CHAPTER 7

"Never be bullied into silence. Never allow yourself to be a victim."
Robert Frost

Bullying is not new. Thanks to child advocates, law enforcement, teachers unions, media, etc., there has been appropriate and intense attention given to bullying in the past several years and I say it's about time.

As we all know there is both physical and emotional bullying. Both leaving scars and both long-lasting.

Why has our society accepted bullying? If you look at our culture throughout the years there is much evidence to support the theory bullying is not only alive and well but had been nourished and healthy for many years.

Movies have glorified different types of bullying in gangster, western and war movies where people are beaten, killed, or otherwise threatened if they don't "do as they are told."

Certain types of music, video games and sporting events have success in sales because of their aggressive image and pitch to people.

Teaching techniques in schools, particularly physical education classes where students are "motivated" by being threatened with additional running, more calisthenics and humiliation, are time-honored in many school districts.

In business and industry employees face threats of losing employment every day for not doing many things unrelated to the job description.

Bullying is a way of life because we allow it. We have made ourselves victims by letting it be acceptable. How many times do we hear the excuse "they were abused as kids?"

My question is, what about the victims? Being silent and allowing ourselves to be victims is what bullies want and what feeds them.

Bullying is anything but acceptable. Bullies use fear as their primary weapon. Overcoming any fear is stressful to say the least.

Once you accept the role of victim it becomes a mindset. You suddenly find yourself continuing to be taken advantage of, continually be emotionally and physically abused.

There is no simple answer. Being a victim to a bully and not reporting it to proper authorities opens you to be a victim in other aspects of life.

Obviously fear of retaliation causes us not to report any assault. But remember that letting yourself be a victim has consequences as well, with the most potent being continually living in fear.

CHAPTER 8

"Stop worrying about who you aren't and start worrying about who you are." John Hagee

There is a saying that goes something like, "don't worry about what other people have just appreciate what you got."

We all at one time or another want something we don't have. It's really not such a bad thing to want but sometimes we let our desire to be someone we're not or push so hard to get something we don't have that we miss out on the joys of being who we are.

Never have I thought it is a bad idea to model yourself after a successful person or want nice things. What can be a bad idea is how you go about it.

I like to ask my students on the first day of class to define themselves. Tell me who they are. I want them to identify their core values as they know them and then tell me if they are happy with who they believe they are.

And that is my point totally with worrying about what you are not rather than worrying about what you are. Core values are key to defining the person. Core values are core for a reason. If you can achieve various goals throughout your life without compromising your core values you are going to live without a lot of unnecessary stress.

When you become so concerned about being like someone else you forget who you are and what you are about, you literally throw your identity away. And many times, you throw not just core values away but friends and family.

I remember someone telling me, "the only thing about fair is it comes once a year." Life isn't fair or it certainly doesn't seem like it at times. But remember the good blessings in your life and strive to make them better. There's nothing wrong with wanting more but don't lose the good you have for the better you may never reach.

CHAPTER 9

"The Power of Belief in Yourself" Lou Tice (and many others)

The story I am going to tell you was first told to me by a mentor of mine who I never met but always respected and feel like I owe a lot of my thinking to. Lou Tice, along with his wife Diane, founded the Pacific Institute out in the Seattle, Washington area. The Pacific Institute is dedicated to using techniques of cognitive therapy to help motivate students, businesses, industries and the military. It is known world-wide for its great success and I have felt privileged to have been associated with them when I was a college professor.

One of the major goals in Lou Tice's life was to make people realize their potential. Lou believed every one of us has potential we don't ever take advantage of. He felt one of the primary reasons we don't take utilize our potential is because we don't believe in ourselves enough.

The following story is based on the movie "The Wizard of Oz." Lou told this story many times in his travels around the world and I'm sure its had various renditions by different people over the years and I felt this would be appropriate for this book so here is Lou's thoughts on what can happen when you realize you have the power to believe in yourself.

The Wizard of Oz - A Different Look

Have you ever thought of the "Wizard of Oz" to strengthen your belief system in yourself?

If you remember the story, Dorothy and her friends all were in search of something and they were looking for someone to give that something to them. They looked for somebody with power, and that's why they were off to see the Wizard. Rather than search alone they began their search together although they were all wanting something different, they knew the Wizard was all powerful and could grant any request. Nothing was thought to be impossible for the Wizard of Oz.

As they journeyed to Oz they also learned a lot about each other and themselves. Finally, as the story climaxes they reach Oz and find the Wizard. After each of them tell the Wizard what they want the Wizard grants the requests. The Cowardly Lion wanted courage. The Wizard gave him a medal rewarding him for his courage. Suddenly the Lion felt courage, he believed he was courageous. The Tin Man wanted a heart and the Wizard gave him a velvet shaped heart filled with sawdust. The Tin Man then believed he had heart. The Scarecrow wanted a brain. The Wizard gave the Scarecrow a diploma with his name on it to show the Scarecrow he could think. The Scarecrow believed he had a brain. Finally, Dorothy just wanted to go home. She didn't know how to ask. And the Wizard took her back home.

Dorothy, the Cowardly Lion, the Tin Man and the Scarecrow all only needed one thing: Belief in themselves. It took simple items to symbolize what all four really knew about themselves but were too low on self-confidence to admit. Actually, in Dorothy's case she had to admit to herself she wanted to go home and leave her friends an Oz. It was a rite of passage into her own strength and heart.

What the characters in the Wizard of Oz found was that they all had the power they were searching for in the first place. What they discovered was they had potential. They already had the power to get what they wanted, they just had to understand their potential to achieve it. Isn't the same thing they were doing what we all need to be doing in real life? Believing in ourselves. We all have unused, undeveloped potential. We have the power to do many things. We just must believe.

CHAPTER 10

"For every reason it's not possible there are hundreds of people who have faced the same circumstances and succeeded." Jack Canfield.

I've learned that many things in life are intense, challenging and time-consuming. These things have caused arguments, fights, even hatred. But what else I've learned is most things aren't impossible.

Meaningful accomplishments and successes, especially if they are worthwhile, are not easily achieved. In fact, it's usually just the opposite.

Circumstances for sure are primary reasons some succeed faster than others. Obviously being "born" into wealth can be key to how you go about dealing with many situations.

On the other side of the coin not having money is just as much a key in how you go about dealing with many situations.

Location, environment, friends, enemies, etc., all play various factors in how problems are resolved.

As pointed out in the quote by Mr. Canfield, many people with the same circumstances are confronted with either same or similar situations every day.

So what is the reason all of these people don't meet with success? Sometimes when solving problems, I like to look at intangibles. One such intangible is desire.

Desire is something not easily measured in quantity. It is evident in what is accomplished and by who. It's also very evident in what's not accomplished and by who.

It's been my experience dealing with students, clients, friends and family that given all things being equal, those who succeed in what they strive to accomplish is a result of desire.

What makes desire more intense with some of us than others? To answer that question, I believe we first need to evaluate our values system. Desire is a bi-product of a quality values system.

I can't stress how often I mention the need for a strong values system in any speaking engagement or in any class I teach. Good values are one of our strongest shields against the challenges of adversity we face. When people face the same problems under the same circumstances, and some succeed while others fail the difference is desire routed in good values.

CHAPTER 11

"Time is the coin of your life. You spend it. Do not allow others to spend it for you." Carl Sandburg

I remember years ago in high school a teacher told us we needed to quit wasting time because it was something we could never get back. Somehow, I really doubt she was that worried about time lost out of our life as much as she was just wanting us to shut up.

When you think about it time is one thing given to us free at birth. Some of us get very little of it while others get decades of it. None of us know when it will end but we all know that one day it will.

We've all heard the saying, "time's money!" Business and industry certainly see it that way. The more production in a certain amount of time the more profit generated for that amount of time.

"Time flies!" Many of us can certainly vouch for that. How many of us can remember when our first child was born while we are watching it graduate from high school or while we're sitting in the waiting room when that first grandchild is born?

Drive through your old neighborhood. Is the house you grew up in still there? Has it been replaced by housing projects or a shopping mall? What about your old school? Is it still there? Memories suddenly are that is left.

I think a lot about time passing by around Memorial Day. When Vicki and I travel to some of the local cemeteries decorating graves.

So time may be the most valuable coin in our life. And we should try to use it wisely. Enjoy time where it matters most with family and friends. Use it efficiently at work and providing for those we love.

Coins of money can be replaced. Coins of time once spent are gone forever.

CHAPTER 12

"When you want to win a game, you have to teach. When you lose
a game, you have to learn." Tom Landry

Maybe it is because I coached for so many years but I've always felt some of the best psychologists and motivators in the world are coaches and teachers.

I'm certain psychologists, professors and counselors beg to disagree and I am privileged to know and call many of them friends and colleagues and can provide excellent arguments for my opinion. As such I would like to make a few following points.

To begin with winning or succeeding, depending on what word you choose, is the result of both teaching and learning.

Successful businesses, athletes, students and coaches all need to learn and learning is the reward of failure. Whether we take advantage of that reward is up to us.

Coaches review game film over and over trying to find at least one weakness in a future opponent and then teach their players how to capitalize on that weakness.

When a team loses a game coaches review that game either using film or charts learning what mistake caused the loss and how to not make that same mistake again.

Isn't the same scenario true in life? We teach our children how to be successful and not make the same mistakes we did. We also learn from our mistakes. Remember the greatest benefit of losing or failing is the ability to learn.

Both the abilities to teach and to learn originate from life. As we are taught from our parents and teachers, we learn to teach our own children.

So teaching and learning have one important element in common. They both feed off motivation. How important is it to you not to make the same mistake twice?

So to my original point. Why are coaches and teachers the best motivators? Could it be enthusiasm. In order to promote any type of motivation you first must display enthusiasm. Then the real trick becomes conveying that enthusiasm to others. Enthusiasm is the critical tool needed to motivate. Coaches and teachers who display enthusiasm in what they are doing automatically convey it to others.

Teaching and learning. To lead you teach. To lead you must demonstrate to those being led you are enthusiastic and care. To learn you must have the enthusiasm to explore and be open to new ideas; to see a failure or loss not as the end but as a challenge to learn for the future.

CHAPTER 13

"The greatest use of your life is to invest in that which outlasts it."
William James

Many people worry about what their legacy will be after they are gone. What are they going to be remembered for.

Some people want their names to be remembered on walls, buildings, scholarships, murals, etc.

Is just having your name survive on some object enough for a legacy? Does the name alone tell your story?

When you invest your life in doing good things for your family, friends or community there is a good chance it won't be forgotten.

True investments in people aren't predicated on future expectations. True investments are not even planned. They happen.

We invest in our children every day. And we most likely don't realize we are doing it. When we teach our kids manners, values, how to care for others, we are not only teaching them we are planting a piece of ourselves. We are investing our beliefs and values in our children and at the same time the future. How well those values and beliefs are instilled and what part they play in how our children develop into adulthood will be an investment that will survive for generations.

Touching lives, making a positive impression, whether your own family's or people you don't or may never know, can be investments that are rich in quality and impossible to measure in longevity.

CHAPTER 14

"No one is useless in this world who lightens the burden of it to anyone else." Charles Dickens

I don't believe anyone is useless in this world regardless of how insignificant they may appear but I do definitely believe anyone who makes this world a little easier to cope with for anyone else is valuable.

Our society has coined a new phrase over the past several years: "it's all about me." This phrase to me describes what my parent's generation called selfishness.

Selfishness is one of the discussions points I talk about with groups when the subject is values.

Our society has moved dramatically from caring about others to only focusing on the individual. Sociologists and psychologists like to blame the advancement of technology, economics and intensity of general family pressures as reasons people today are only concerned if it concerns them.

I like to believe helping others is a positive quality. I try to instill in my children and grandchildren the simple ways to be helpful: holding a door open for someone, saying good morning or thank you regardless of whether there is a reply, just smiling at someone.

To me it really doesn't matter if those I try to help or be courteous to even acknowledge me. I know it. I feel good that I have done something for someone. Helping anyone in a positive way can't help but jump start your own day.

I really believe if you can lighten someone's load in this world, even for a few minutes, you are anything but useless, indeed you are valuable!

CHAPTER 15

"If you can go through life without experiencing pain you haven't been born yet." Neil Simon

Pain is something that comes in so many forms and has no prejudice about who it affects.

Whether physical or emotional, pain leaves scars. Some of those scars heal while some never do.

I think it's fair to say most emotional scars are more lasting than physical. Someone who falls and breaks a bone may be in pain for a few weeks but someone who has experienced betrayal of a close friend, spouse or other family member may be emotionally hurt for years.

Most likely pain of some type has been experienced by all of us within the first year of life. The severity of pain, whether physical or emotional, has much to do with its consequences.

While physical pain can be frequently controlled or eliminated within a reasonable time depending upon severity of the injury or condition, emotional pain can survive for years or even a lifetime and increase in intensity.

How we cope with any type of pain in our lives determines the quality of life we will have.

Although it is virtually impossible to go through life without experiencing pain it is certainly possible to control pain throughout life and not let it control us.

CHAPTER 16

"I've always made a total effort, even when the odds seemed entirely against me. I never quit trying; I never felt I didn't have a chance to win." Arnold Palmer

Sometimes I wonder if everyone of us at one time or another feel like everything is against us.

The chances are we have all experienced a moment in time when we felt the deck was totally stacked. Particularly we feel helpless when we want something special and every attempt, we make to get it fails for whatever reason.

Beating the odds is a continual dream of gamblers. The bigger the risk the bigger the possible payoff. Always believing you will win and cash in sooner than later.

When I was coaching the most important point stressed in every practice and game was to never quit, never give up.

I've found that there are some people who start getting stronger as the stress or pressure gets greater. History is full of stories about battles and wars won by people who had their "backs to the wall."

There's many stories about people who have been deathly sick, weak and thought to be hopeless but then suddenly they make amazing recoveries. Some then go on to make major contributions to life.

I think Arnold Palmer said it best, "I never felt I didn't have a chance to win."

Regardless of the steep challenges we face in life and all the many obstacles we have to overcome, there is always a chance for success if we don't quit.

People walk out of hospitals every day ready to once again take on life because they believed they would regain their health. Students graduate with degrees and move on to high-paying jobs because they don't get frustrated and quit over school assignments and people beat drugs and alcohol addiction because they don't give up and win in the difficult world of recovery.

So it comes down to not just how much you want something but how you have nurtured your character. Just as losing and quitting can be a dangerous habit, fighting the good fight and dealing with roadblocks and obstacles leading to a successful life can be characteristics of a happy and productive person.

CHAPTER 17

"Think of giving not as a duty but as a privilege." John D. Rockefeller

One of my greatest blessings was my parents' attitude towards helping others. Both mom and dad would always put themselves out to help anyone.

I remember every summer we would give away most everything in our garden to the neighbors and just about anyone else who wanted something. Years later I realized most of the stuff we planted none of us ate to begin with. My parents just raised the vegetables to give to others but we never realized it then. Mom used to can green beans, tomatoes, corn and give most of it away to neighbors.

My brother and I were always told to shovel snow in the neighbors driveways, mow the grass for neighbors too old to do it themselves and to always offer to help anytime we thought it was needed.

Looking back I can say it was my first introduction to the concept of giving. It's one of the greatest values my parents ever gave me.

I attribute the desire for most of my public service work to those days growing up on Pleasant Avenue. I've always felt helping others should still have the same priority in my life today as it did when growing up.

The rewards for giving are invaluable for me. Through my work with Kiwanis, the Autism Project of Southern Ohio, little league, youth soccer and other endeavors I have always considered it a privilege to give my time and energy.

I have been privileged to meet so many wonderful people and participate in so many great activities and enjoy every minute of it especially knowing others are benefitting.

My parents believed giving and helping others is a privilege. They felt good helping others and I feel great helping others.

I like to believe God put us all here for different reasons. We all have callings. God has given me the opportunity to be in position to give and help others. He let my parents instill in me the desire to give.

In my life I am so thankful I have been given the opportunity and privilege to help others and to reap the rewards it brings.

CHAPTER 18

"Life isn't about finding yourself. Life is about creating yourself."
George Bernard Shaw

Anyone who has been at one of my lectures or read anything I've written knows I put a lot of emphasis on personality development, building positive self-esteem and being success oriented. Key to all of this is the ability to create yourself.

A point I try to drive home often is the individual doesn't have to be satisfied with who he or she currently is but can create the person they want to be.

I like to think that creating who we are is a life-long process called growing.

When we hear the phrase "finding yourself," it implies you are realizing what values, morals, and general lifestyle you are living. "Finding yourself "does not mean you are happy with yourself and your life.

When an individual decides to create themselves there must also be a commitment to change. It's easy to say you are creating a new life, changing attitudes, friends, overall environment. The commitment to not relapse to the "former you" are the determining factor in creating a "new you." Creating a new life is half the challenge while living the life makes it real.

Growth is the result of creating a life that is productive, goal oriented and flexible enough to look at new ideas and new concepts with an open mind and acceptance of others for who they are not who you want them to be.

CHAPTER 19

"Ten seconds of silence for ten people who cared and helped shape your life." Fred Rogers.

Fred Rogers asked everyone while accepting an Emmy Award to "take ten seconds of silence and think of ten people who cared and helped shape your life."

Rogers went on to ask how proud those people might be to know they were thought of so highly and considered so important in another person's life.

We all can think of people who were major influences in our lives, either positively or negatively.

Those who unfortunately influenced us negatively are most likely some of the people we probably think of more frequently. Negative experiences tend to make longer lasting impressions on our minds. Negative events affect us emotionally, physically and socially. They cause loss of self-confidence, withdrawal from relationships, lack of sleep and various health issues.

In order to think frequently about those who have helped guide our lives positively we need to have what I call an attitude of gratitude.

If we are grateful for the positive happenings in our lives we can't help but recognize those who supported us along the way. And if we are grateful, we don't forget where we were or where we are now.

CHAPTER 20

"In reading the lives of great men, I have found that the first victory they have won is over themselves." Harry S. Truman

Remember the saying, "you are your own worst enemy"? Many of us have been told that at one time or another.

Some people have what is referred to as a "inner drive." It's a passion or obsession, depending on what description you use but it's really an internal battle to always be the best. Successful athletes, doctors, lawyers, leaders in business and industry many times drive themselves so hard they put family and relationships on a back burner.

There are many who fight "demons" within their minds caused by drugs, alcohol or even environment. Their inner drive is what keeps them moving forward.

History is full of stories of people who have overcome obstacles that could have overcame them. One man was President of the United States while restricted to a wheelchair. Many recovering addicts and alcoholics are some of the finest counselors you will ever meet. And look at the high success rate of many disabled American veterans in our workforce. All these people have won battles against themselves.

It's fair to say that before you lead others you first have to be able to lead yourself. Getting your own act together is necessary before you can expect others to do the same.

The phrase "any man can father a child but not every man can be a father" is a good example of needing to get your own life together or winning the battle against yourself before you take on other battles.

CHAPTER 21

"However difficult life may seem there is always something you can do and succeed at." Stephen Hawking

An honor I've been privileged to have several times in my life is being key-note speaker at several graduation ceremonies.

In every one of those messages I have delivered the underlying theme is we all have something we will be successful at although it may take some of us a little longer to find it than others.

One of the most dramatic times in anyone's life is the day you walk on the graduation stage as a student and walk off as a successful graduate with the world waiting on you.

It's at that point when you realize that you're on your own that reality sits in. Sometimes I think it's our first reality check.

Frustration is most likely the hardest thing to deal with when you are trying to figure out what your life is going to be like.

The other big thing you find out about yourself as you move through life is that life isn't going to usually give you what you think you want. How you handle that realization determines how successful you will become.

Finally it's important not to be so rigid in your schedule to become a success. Rigidity breeds frustration. You have to understand that life is synonymous with flexibility.

Certainly there are those who appear to reach success quickly and that's great. But their challenge is to stay successful. For others the journey to success is a difficult road. But there is something there for all of us if we stay the course.

CHAPTER 22

"That's what we're here on this Earth for, to help others." Betty Ford

When I think about Betty Ford's quote I always ask myself, "why wouldn't we all not want to help others."

My parents always told both Jerry and me growing up that anytime you have the chance to help anyone, do it, because you never know when the day will come you will need help.

I believe the greatest thing about helping others is it shows you are not a selfish individual totally wrapped up in yourself. It's what I always refer to as the "all about me" syndrome.

Sometimes I think people get the impression that the only help you can give people is with money. I tend to believe giving money is likely the least productive way to help others.

Helping can be looked at in various ways. You can help others emotionally, physically, spiritually as well as financially.

Emotional help or support can never be measured. Folks who are emotionally hurting don't necessarily need money to solve the hurt. They want and need someone to listen to them, to talk to them and to know they will be there.

Helping physically can obviously take on many scenarios. From simple things such as cutting a friend's grass or shoveling snow in a neighbor's driveway to holding a car door open are all small ways to help but extremely appreciated. Helping people who have emergency needs such fixing a flat tire or repairing a water pipe in someone's basement to watching someone's children after school because they suddenly had to work a double shift are just more examples of physically helping people in need.

Being a spiritual friend to someone is of tremendous help. From a standpoint of faith it is of major value to have someone to talk with, pray with, pray for and know they are praying for you.

In closing I would say that no matter what type of help you may give someone it is always important to remember that a day could easily come when you may need the very same help. So why wouldn't you want to help others?

CHAPTER 23

"Challenges are what makes life interesting and overcoming them is what makes life meaningful." Joshua J. Marine

No one could be blamed for thinking life is a challenge.

Indeed there are few of us who could say with total honesty we haven't faced some challenges throughout our lives.

When you look at the many different types of challenges faced during a lifetime: health, finance, spiritual, relationship, etc., there is no one common way to cope with each other than with a positive attitude.

Many examples of challenges that may never have been overcome if not for a positive attitude can be cited. I think of the great positive attitude our country had after being brutally attacked at Pearl Harbor. How the great positive attitude the United States showed the world as it crushed the Axis Powers proved any challenge could be overcome if persistence and perseverance were coupled with a refusal to accept any negativity.

The great positive attitude of children fighting cancer and other debilitating diseases, the positive attitude our disabled veterans display as they put their lives back together after suffering traumatic and life-long injuries while fighting to keep our country safe.

And there is the positive attitude of families who have lost loved ones to addiction, vehicle accidents and senseless killings.

The world is full of challenges. We can either attack the challenge with a positive attitude and find ways to eliminate the problem or we can retreat into our secure comfort zone and let the problem control us.

CHAPTER 24

"No matter what you've done for yourself or for humanity, if you can't look back on having given love and attention to your own family, what have you really accomplished?" Lee Iacocca

It seems today much of our society has gotten its priorities completely out of order.

When I teach or speak at events I always like to talk about priorities and how values should play a primary part of your decision making.

The message I like to get across is the values you develop are the values that will guide your life. So, you need to remember a key point about success: the values that motivate you to success will most likely be the values you maintain success with.

I was fortunate to be raised believing family and God are first. We were not a regular attending church going family. But we all developed values regarding right and wrong, fairness, respect and love.

I'm happy to say as I have went through life any success I have attained came with those values being the framework.

Family and God have been and still are the foundation of my values. I've tried so very hard throughout life to do everything not only for myself but my family.

Today I can't say everything I've done has worked out for them, but I can say my family were and will always be part of any decision. As much as I enjoy working, meeting people and trying to help with different charities and causes, it would all be an empty feeling without going home to my family each night.

There are so many people I have met over the years that are more successful than I will ever be professionally but many of them are alone, maybe they're married and have kids, but there is no connection. The success road bi-passed home. The family wasn't part of it. For sure they benefitted but they didn't share because the values system of the one didn't allow for the inclusion of all.

To me accomplishments are to be shared and enjoyed by those I care about most. I can honestly say in one way or another every accomplishment, every success, wouldn't be as meaningful without my family and friends sharing.

CHAPTER 25

"Circumstances may cause interruptions and delays, but never lose sight of your goals." Mario Andretti

How many of us can say that we haven't been interrupted in one way or another as we go through life?

As we grow so comes more challenges. Challenges cause detours in life. How we approach those challenges determines whether we reach our goals or alter them.

Part of setting goals involves the realization that if they are goals worthy of achieving they are not going to be easy to attain.

When I talk about goal setting I like to tell people to set whatever goals they want. Set them as high as they want and then develop a plan to achieve them. But I also say to be flexible in their journey.

We grow as we work toward goal setting.

Part of growth is adjusting not necessarily accepting. Some of the greatest achievements in our history are the result of goals that took years to achieve, one obstacle after another, frustration after frustration.

What is the secret to achieving goals. I like to think it is persistence in not taking your eye off the prize coupled with a understanding that flexibility in how you get the prize is essential.

Remember, great plans; i.e. business, military and life plans all have flexibility for dealing with obstacles and interruptions. The key is being flexible in dealing with the circumstances as they arise, stay persistent and keep your eye on the prize.

CHAPTER 26

"Try not to become a man of success. Rather become a man of value." Albert Einstein

There are those that point to successful people and immediately assume them to be of integrity and value as all three must go together.

Certainly many successful people would not have become that way without having value in their lives. But to assume being a person of success is synonymous with value is not exactly accurate.

I think there are certain requirements to be a person of value. One such requirement is being able to make other people realize they are valuable. In other words adding value to another person's life.

How long has it taken you to realize you are a person of value, or do you feel you have value?

Many times it takes others to make us aware of our best features. There are many who never consider their own value. Unfortunately, I think there are many who go to their graves never realizing how valuable a person they were.

In order to be a person of value it is essential to make others feel they too are valuable. Making other people feel important, having worth, is critical in our own value.

One other requirement to be a person of value is keeping our word. Our word is the greatest reflection of who we are as a person.

Success is as they say, "in the eye of the beholder." It is possible to have a successful life, good job, good family and comfortable life style but still not have a life of value.

There are countless stories about successful men and women who appear on the surface to have the world at their "finger tips," but in reality are sad even miserable people. Some of these people end up their lives being alone, miserable or in some instances ending their lives.

I attribute not having any value to these people's lives as the primary reason for their misery. Not being valued by others and not having any value for yourself presents an overwhelming depression and emptiness that no amount of success by itself can conquer.

CHAPTER 27

"We build too many walls and not enough bridges." Sir Isaac Newton

As far as we have come in our society throughout the years there are still areas that need lots of improvement.

Stigmas continue to plague our culture. Most of my professional career has been spent working with special needs populations and folks suffering from addictions and mental health issues.

I have continually been amazed over the years how people who should know better, so called "professionals," still place stigmas on others. They put up these walls that imply wanting to be shielded from what or who they feel "better" than.

It's my feeling that stigmas are not on those they are directed at but rather those who demonstrate their self-assumed superiority. These people reflect a personality in need of continual approval, power and control.

History records many different events and periods where some people were looked at as somehow inferior. They were treated with pity, ridicule and cruelty.

Stigmas are a cancer on our society. They are contagious and are just as prevalent with the rich as the poor.

Stigmas come in all sizes and colors: Money (or lack of), age, size, race, disability, even divorced or single parents.

I've never understood why in a world where we can make a bomb strong enough to destroy civilizations or put a man on the moon, that we build such walls between ourselves.

I can honestly say I've been very proud to share my life with people who have come from many different facets of life. I hate the idea of walls between people. Senseless stigmas that achieve nothing other than cause hurt to innocent people trying to live in the same world and face the same struggles can only be eliminated by maturity, common sense and a deep appreciation for our blessings.

CHAPTER 28

"Be always at war with your vices, at peace with your neighbors,
and let each new year find you a better person." Benjamin Franklin

Internal turmoil is common to everyone. There is no one living or dead that hasn't experienced some internal strife at one time or another. Actually in some cases internal worry or grief has led people to stomach ulcers, heart attacks and death.

We human beings each deal differently with the world around us. We all know people who seem to not have a care in the world. They are always smiling, laughing and happy. Then one day you hear on the radio or read in the newspaper where they have died sometimes tragically. There are also times where these same types of people turn up in rehab clinics or hospitals suffering from some type of addiction or mental health issue.

I agree with Benjamin Franklin that we need to be always aware of our surroundings. We do need to be at war with our vices. Just as we need to be at peace with our neighbors, family and friends.

What Franklin didn't emphasize was how we should cope with this everlasting responsibility. Being at war with our emotions and vices is in many ways a 24-hour seven day a week effort. Internal turmoil in our lives doesn't sleep so we don't rest.

Coping with our vices on a day to day basis can best be accomplished by not ignoring their existence. Realizing what the issues are that trouble us in life and admitting to ourselves they indeed are a problem is the first step in dealing with them.

Developing and implementing a plan to cope with the daily vices of life is the best way to wage the war Franklin talks about. Remember wars are won only by first winning battles. Winning a battle each day against a vice brings you closer to winning the war.

Peace is the goal of life. With it comes happiness, contentment and deep appreciation for the world around us. It is virtually impossible to have peace with neighbors and friends without having inner peace.

Finding inner peace, controlling our emotions and fighting vices are great goals to begin any year. Living in peace, happy and fulfilled, is the goal of a lifetime.

CHAPTER 29

"What would life be if we had no courage to attempt anything?"
Vincent Van Gogh

What is courage? How do you define the word courage?

Several years ago John F. Kennedy wrote a best-seller, "Profiles in Courage," profiling people he considered to have demonstrated great courage in their lives.

Courage can have many examples: people who climb mountains, those who parachute from airplanes, drive race cars at unbelievable high rates of speed, and those who chase tornadoes to gage their potential impact.

There's also the tremendous courage of our American military, police, fire and emergency response personnel.

We can also see courage in the eyes of young children suffering from terminal illnesses and the remarkable struggles of their families. Also, we find courage in the spirit of those people who see their homes and lives uprooted due to the horrible fires, hurricanes, earthquakes and other natural disasters throughout the world.

Courage can be seen in so many places by so many people in so many ways. There is no doubt courage is a characteristic of a positive self-image.

Courage like many other attributes a person may have needs to be utilized with wisdom.

Although many and various situations faced in life may require courage at one point there needs to be a realization that courage used positively can reap great rewards while courage used poorly or boastfully can only reap disaster.

We could say courage is a motivator to cause people to do good things and make good decisions. Responsibility is also necessary in order to utilize courage positively. Responsibility and courage need to go hand in hand.

Courage is a great quality. But courage needs to be coupled with common sense and responsibility for our actions resulting from a courageous act to be valuable.

CHAPTER 30

"The only competition that matters is the one that takes place within yourself." Pete Carroll

For most successful people, regardless of their profession, the strongest competitor they have in life is themselves.

As a former coach I've found my best players may have needed fundamentals or strategic coaching but very little motivational coaching.

When it came to competing in the game you could see the determination in their eyes. The motivation was already there but it wasn't the competition they were playing; it was the competition within themselves to be the best and be the winner.

Successful businesspeople are their own fiercest competitors as well. The passion within their own minds to make the right deals, sell the most, have the highest production, it all comes from the pressure from within themselves. Every business man or woman wants to be the best at what they do but it's that inner drive that separates the best from the rest.

So it's safe to say the motivational spirit or will that is internal in many people is the only fuel they most likely will ever need in moving toward successful goals. True, encouragement and congratulations on various achievements will reinforce their internal fires but it's never as strong as the competition from within.

One of my favorite mentors, John Maxwell, says, "successful and unsuccessful people do not vary greatly in their abilities. They vary in their desires to reach their potential."

I believe there's a lot of truth in that comment. Abilities can be improved on, fine-tuned, but then comes the intangible: the desire and the competition from within to make the abilities work successfully toward a desired goal.

No matter what goals we may set in life, no matter how difficult, no matter how many people we have to compete against, our hardest competition will come against ourselves. Proving to ourselves we can achieve something, fighting the obstacles and not giving in to the challenge is the real fight. And the real opponent is us.

CHAPTER 31

"Stop letting people who do so little for you control so much of your mind, feelings and emotions." Will Smith

Have you ever heard someone say, "she's too good for him, or he can do a lot better than her?"

Many people have a tendency in life to let others influence them usually in ways that are non-productive and detrimental.

Those who do this manipulating of others are themselves very insecure, have low self-esteem, are paranoid and are full of negativity. The only time these people are happy is when they are dragging others into their own self-made misery.

It is imperative that people working toward a positive successful life avoid this type of behavior. People who do this manipulation prey on those who they perceive to be weak in character and uncertain of where they want their lives to lead.

Once you let someone control your emotions and feelings they also control your relationships, your work habits and even what you eat and when you sleep.

There's an old saying, "misery loves company." I taught night classes at one time composed of people who had to work during the day but took courses at night to eventually get a better job. They had a positive self-image and a plan to move their lives forward.

What happened in several cases was so-called friends tried every possible way to get these students to drop out or miss class often. It was a way to manipulate. These "friends" felt they were losing control.

I always told my students to be cautious of those who tried to steer you away from your goals. They are not looking out for you but rather themselves. They want the control of knowing you are as miserable as they are but are terrified you will escape their life of insecurity.

Unfortunately for most of us we tend to develop relationships that become more beneficial for the other person. It's really a test of maturity as we not only realize these people are manipulating us, but we also have to develop the courage to turn them away from our lives.

Letting others control our emotions, thoughts and feelings is not living. It is existing. Remember in order to live a life of success and happiness you must live your life your way.

CHAPTER 32

"Associate with those who help you believe in yourself." Brooks Robinson

When I was growing up my parents used to always tell me, "you are judged by the company you keep." I didn't realize the impact of that statement until years later but today I've discovered it was prophetic.

If you look back in life I think most of us could remember one or more people we probably would have been better off not having in our social circle.

What I've found is a lot of our friends are only our friends until they can't use us anymore. Once that happens they turn on us, usually through vengeance and jealousy.

People who constantly attack the self-esteem and character of others themselves have low self-esteem, little or no confidence and only can feed their own egos by downgrading the success, accomplishments and positive future of others.

So what can we do? People you know who are constantly trying to hold you back and bring you down must be removed from your life socially and professionally immediately.

I have told my college freshmen students many times that once they've committed themselves to pursuing their degrees they will see their friends from high school days slowly pull away from them. Their lives will no longer have common ground. As the friends watch your continued education cause you to take on new direction both socially and professionally there will be less and less involvement together.

Some of your friends will actually encourage you but in most cases the majority will not only discourage you they will also develop untruths about why your relationship has changed. Most of these reasons will be based on unfounded jealousy and excuses for not trying to improve their own lives.

So as it is vitally important to phase out those from your life that discourage your personal development it is also just as important to realize this is not your fault those people have "turned". You have done nothing wrong. You have made both a life and career decision to improve yourself and family. It's called maturity and accepting the responsibilities of life.

CHAPTER 33

"There is no shame in changing course when aiming for success".
Robert Herjavec

It's always been interesting to me that we expect young people to make career decisions before they graduate from high school.

When school kids get to their senior year, and sometimes before, they have made critical life decisions they have had little time to prepare for and unaware of potential career interests that may exist.

These young people have taken college entrance exams, declared majors and scheduled their first day of college, complete with student loans and built-in debt. All before high school graduation.

The same scenario is played out over and over in life by most of us. Whether it is college enrollment or some other career choice we make, many times we decide these choices not really being prepared for that particular career or even wanting to stay in that field.

It's fair to say most of our career decisions are either made for us by others, i.e. parents, teachers, friends or by the need to get a paycheck coming in.

We really do the same thing with relationships. We go into relationships not knowing what we really want but only that we feel pressured from friends, family and co-workers to be in one.

Then just like ending up in a profession we are not interested in or successful in, we also end up in relationships we are not happy or successful at.

Sadly many people spend their lives in careers and relationships for the wrong reasons. They are not happy but feel trapped and in some ways they are.

There is nothing wrong with starting over. Especially when you know you are where you don't want to be in a situation: career or relationship. As with any decision there are consequences. Change breeds consequences.

I always advise students and clients to not start over in any endeavor unless they know why they can't go further. To not know why you are starting over and still try to change course will most likely only bring you back to the same place you are already at. Starting over is dramatic both physically and emotionally. And sometimes starting over and going in a different direction involves more than you. Friends and family come into play. Some aren't going to be happy because indirectly their lives are being affected also.

But I encourage you to live your life in the direction you want it to go. You may be sharing your life with many, but you are living it for yourself. God made all of us unique from each other and blessed us by letting us choose the direction we want to go. It's a blessing you shouldn't waste.

CHAPTER 34

"But what is happiness except the simple harmony between a man and the life he leads." Albert Camus.

How do you define happiness? And a follow-up question is, what does it take to make you happy?

Those two questions are most likely asked more than any question other than "how are you", on any given day and yet there's rarely a thoughtful answer.

Priorities definitely have a key role in what defines happiness for people. As we grow, we normally mature. And as we mature our values become solidified.

One important thought to keep in mind is how you compare happiness to contentment. While many people equate happiness to security, a great retirement and some type of "financially secure future" for their children, others are only happy when they are looking for that next great challenge. Those people have a totally different concept of life. Not that they care about their families any less they just thrive on challenging the unknown. They are not necessarily careless or irresponsible but just have a different outlook on life. To these people happiness is the next challenge in life.

I look at happiness as a life-long process. I know my priorities have changed both personally and professionally over the years. There were many things that made me happy years ago that I really have little use for today. And today there are things I never dreamed about before that I couldn't imagine not having in my life now. Will that change? I don't know.

Happiness does have to be in harmony with a person's life. Contentment with your lifestyle is critical for happiness. But as human beings we must remember one of our blessings is we have the ability to change our minds, our attitudes and yes, our values. Make sure that as you go through life you don't confuse happiness with convenience. Be sure you are living a happy life not just content with a life of convenience.

CHAPTER 35

"Success is more permanent when you achieve it without destroying your principles." Walter Cronkite

There is no question that true success must be earned. Earned can be done in a variety of ways, depending on what you want, how much you want and what you are willing to do to get it.

I prefer to look at success in positive terms, i.e. having a good job, friends and great family. Others look at success in terms of power, money and fame. Still others see success only through manipulation and intimidation required to get what they want.

For success to be worthwhile it must be sustainable. Success that is fleeting isn't really success it is just temporary gratification.

Principles and values are fundamental to the foundation for our lives. If we have principles based on cheating, stealing and stepping on others to move "up the latter," we may achieve what we want but will only be able to sustain it if we use the same attitudes and methods. That type of success will only last if we want to be subservient to paranoia, jealousy and anxiety which comes with principles based on selfishness and dishonesty. Eventually any success achieved will slip away as it cannot be genuine.

If you choose to obtain success through values and principles based on common decency, fairness and a strong work ethic the results can't help but be long-lasting.

Developing good principles and values to live by and then strengthening them as you mature will make your life successful and meaningful in whatever endeavor you choose.

CHAPTER 36

"Show respect even to people who don't deserve it; not as a reflection of their character but as a reflection of yours." Dave Willis

I have come to believe that the majority of many of society's problems involve respect or more specifically lack of respect.

Today there appears to be not nearly as much emphasis on respecting others as in years past. I firmly believe everyone you show respect to, whether they deserve it or not, will respect you in some way. The fact they respect you is not nearly as important as the respect you gain for yourself.

Today's society places much emphasis on the "what's in it for me" attitude. In other words, if there is nothing in a given situation or relationship that benefits someone personally then they want nothing to do with it and there is no respect. Additionally, there seems to be a huge disrespect for all forms of authority, from parental to law enforcement to government.

It's important to point out that in order to respect others and have them respect you that you first must have self-respect. Self-respect comes from having values, goals and a purpose.

For whatever reason our society has put respect on a "back burner" in recent years. As our country and world faces crisis after crisis it's imperative we work together in a collaborative way and the key to successful collaboration is mutual respect.

CHAPTER 37

"HOPE....possibly the most effective of all four-letter words."
Mike Payton.

In this time of uncertainty and confusion, most of us are searching for some type of reassurance that things are going to get better and we will all be ok, that some form of normal will return.

In desperate times, people search both internally and externally for answers. Many people turn to God and different forms of spirituality. Others look to alcohol, drugs, crime, and even suicide in trying to find comfort and escape.

What keeps all of us from "giving up" on life and all the pitfalls that come with it is hope? It's a simple four-letter word but yet it's power Is unbelievably strong.

I look at hope as the heart of positive thinking. In order to hope a person must use positive thinking.

Believing something will happen is hope and hope is fueled by positive thinking: Believing something will happen, situations will change, bad will get better. It all revolves on the hope we have in our minds: the belief something will change and usually for the better.

History is full of stories where the human spirit appears to be totally crushed and yet some strong motivational force appears to change the course into a positive and productive outcome. Pearl Harbor, 9-1-1, the COVID-19, and many more terrifying and challenging events over our history have pushed people's minds and spirit to the potential limit but something has triggered comeback after comeback.

Hope is the motivating factor in life. Whether we gain our hope from God or from another source, there is no question something triggers our inner self to achieve more than we ever thought.

CHAPTER 38

"Never let the fear of striking out get in your way." Babe Ruth

How many times has the fear of not doing something right stopped you from doing it at all?

If you look at some of the great inventors of the world you have to ask yourself what would have happened if:

(1) Thomas Edison gave up after his first try at inventing the light bulb
(2) Alexander Fleming gave up before discovering penicillin
(3) Benjamin Franklin quit before finally discovering electricity

If these three alone had stopped for fear of failing or never even started, think what our world would be like today. History would have to be re-written if the fear of failing prevailed in these and other similar situations.

Fear itself is a natural emotion. Our ability to control it in ourselves has much to do with how we live. Other emotions are the same: to love, hate, how we mourn, rejoice. How we control these emotions or how we let them control us determine our lifestyle.

Keep in mind there is both good fear and bad fear. For example, good fear is the type that keeps us from sticking a finger in an electrical socket or not driving our car the opposite way on a one-way street. Our fear of tornadoes and hurricanes causes us to make certain preparations if we live in areas where they routinely occur.

Bad fear however is what many times holds us back from success. Fear of being laughed at for failing at something: learning to play a musical instrument, learning to swim or even fear of asking someone you like out on a date.

How many people do you know who don't even apply for a job because they are afraid of being turned down? Then there are those who won't try to enroll in college because they don't want to be embarrassed in front of their friends by possibly getting turned down.

Fear can be paralyzing. It can stop us dead in our tracks. It will confine our lives to a comfort zone we will never dare to leave because of the unknown.

Fear can be good. It can keep us from taking unnecessary risks, doing things that can cause harm and present danger.

Remember to control fear and not let fear control you.

CHAPTER 39

"Take one day at a time. Remember today is the tomorrow you worried about yesterday." Billy Graham

Several years ago, there used to be a television show, "One Day at a Time." It was about a divorcee and her two teenage girls trying to face life's obstacles each day. The show was fun to watch but it did have an underlying theme: take life one day at a time.

We spend a lot more of our time each day worrying than we realize. Actually, we spend a lot more time asleep worrying than we know. Restless sleep, tossing and turning, it all is forms of worry.

In our hectic world we spend as much time worrying about getting through today as we do worry about getting through tomorrow.

I believe stress breeds stress. The intensity of worry affects us not just mentally but physically. Instead of coping with stress associated with today we double that intensity when we worry about tomorrow as well.

So how do we take it one day at a time? For one we need to slow down. I'm a big believer in quiet time. In my case I like to get up each morning early, say a little prayer, read a short devotional and drink a cup of coffee. This is my little routine that helps me get focused on my day. I'm not saying everyone should do what I do or even when I do it but I am saying everyone needs to take some time alone each day to get focused.

I've found that getting myself focused on what I'm supposed to do and where I'm supposed to be given me some structure and the few minutes of quiet time gets my mind relaxed and settled.

Handling the events of each day without worrying about tomorrow makes me more relaxed, productive and certainly more pleasant to be around.

Finally, I think we need to line up our priorities. Every day we need to focus on that day's priorities. Some priorities are daily: getting our kids off to school, heading to work, our job itself, then getting supper, dealing with kid's activities (ballgames, etc.). Other priorities need to then fit in to the daily schedule such as doctor's appointments, paying bills, shopping.

Tomorrow may or may not come. But we are here today. Enjoy today. Reap its rewards. Smile, laugh, even cry when you need to. Enjoy your kids and realize your blessings.

Remember that all worrying about tomorrow really does is take away today.

CHAPTER 40

"We have to play out the hand we get in life, deal with the challenges and move forward." Mike Payton

A saying I will never forget hearing from a coach once was, "the only thing about fair is it comes once a year." What he was telling us was no matter how much we want to believe everything about life is fair, the reality is nothing could be further from the truth.

As a person of faith, I do believe God lets us all be born with certain talents and interests which we develop throughout our lifetime. I believe we all achieve our development through experiences in our environment and relationships.

There are intangibles that play into how our lives form. For example, location. If you are born in a rural area and raised in farm communities, you are going to be exposed to a different lifestyle than if you were raised in a metropolitan area.

The same goes for your family. If your family is financially secure you are going to be exposed to a different lifestyle than if you were raised in a low income or poverty-stricken childhood.

The key isn't about what's fair and what's not. It's all about what you do with what you must work with. It comes down to desire and effort. There are many successful people who grew up in split families, little or no money and worked their way through college doing any job they could find.

Also there are people who were born with what you might call a "silver spoon" in their mouths: wealth, wanting for nothing. Today many of them are behind bars, ruined marriages, bankruptcy, alcohol and drug dependent.

Health is also an obstacle in life that isn't always fair. While some are born into great health, become world class athletes and appear the picture of strength and success they still must manage their lives. However, as many do very well financially and socially there are others who become obsessed with themselves, ignore relationships, begin to take advantage of their success and abuse the very gift of health they were God given. Steroid abuse coupled with other physical and mental stresses, usually self-imposed, result in many of these people spending their final days in rehabilitation clinics and even nursing homes miserable and alone, sadly never understanding what happened and blaming everyone else.

There are also people born with immediate health issues or develop them at a young age. Some of these people live what appears to certainly be difficult and demanding lives but yet they may have made themselves models of what success can be using what God gave them and making it work: doctors, lawyers, inventors, authors and even world leaders. Was it hard? Yes. But these people worked with the hand they were dealt. They faced the challenges, stayed the course and showed us lessons about what life is really all about.

We all must accept the hand we are dealt in life initially but that doesn't mean we have to be complacent with it. We can move forward and yes, it most times is a difficult thing to do. Instead of folding, play your hand. Don't try to deal from the bottom of the deck.

CHAPTER 41

"Effort and desire are qualities required to climb the mountain of life." Mike Payton

Nobody ever said life was going to be easy. Who was the last person to say that to you? I would be willing to bet that everyone of us has had that statement made to us at least once in the last year. There also is the very distinct possibility that you have made that statement to someone recently as well.

Today I had the opportunity to watch on television as Queen Elizabeth addressed the citizens of England on the struggles the world is currently going through with the COVID-19 (Coronavirus). Talk about a person who has climbed some mountains of life in her time. She lived through Hitler's bombing of England, several other military conflicts, the economic crises of Europe, the tragic death of Princess Diana, and recently watching as one of her grandsons pretty much left the royal family. Now she, like rest of the world, is trying to provide encouragement and hope to her country during this world-wide pandemic.

For sure others, possibly yourself, have faced many mountains in life and realized how difficult climbing the mountain is. And that mountain of life can involve so many obstacles: health, finance, children, parents, marital relationships, employment.

Jerry Lewis did a telethon to raise money for muscular dystrophy on Labor Day many years. He used to talk about the mountains these young children were forced to climb in life through no fault of their own and he used to sing a song at the end of each show, "You'll Never Walk Alone." The song, at least to me, made the statement that life isn't always easy for many of us and for many, life is even more difficult.

What we are going through now with the COVID-19 is indeed a mountain we are being forced to climb. Unfortunately, it will not be the last mountain to climb. As we go through life, we will face many more mountains, our children and grandchildren will be forced to climb mountains long after we are gone. How successful they will be depending upon the effort and desire they display. For now, we must put forth our most intense efforts and display our strongest desire to climb this mountain.

As was stated earlier, nobody ever said life was going to be easy. I suppose the greatest motivating force is the desire to reach the top of this mountain and then find another one to climb. But then again, maybe that's what life is all about, climbing one mountain after another, never being content in one comfort zone but striving to expand our knowledge and our abilities.

Printed in the United States
by Baker & Taylor Publisher Services